IS-288.A: The Role of Voluntary Organizations in Emergency Management

By

Fema

2/12/2015

Administrative Information 1
   THE FEDERAL EMERGENCY MANAGEMENT AGENCY (FEMA) 1
   EMERGENCY MANAGEMENT INSTITUTE (EMI) 1
  COURSE OVERVIEW 1
   Target Audience 1
   Course Goals and Objectives 2
  PURPOSE OF THIS COURSE 2
   Course Organization 4

Unit One: Overview and History of Voluntary Organizations in
Emergency Management 1-1
  INTRODUCTION 1-1
  UNIQUE STRENGTHS OF VOLUNTARY ORGANIZATIONS................................ 1-1
  THE ROLE OF VOLUNTARY ORGANIZATIONS IN HISTORICAL DISASTERS 1-4
  SUMMARY OF UNIT ONE.. 1-4

Unit Two: Roles and Services of Voluntary Organizations in
Emergency Management 2-1
  INTRODUCTION 2-1
  ROLES OF THE VOLUNTARY SECTOR 2-1
   Sec. 403. Essential Assistance (42 U.S.C. 5170b) 2-2
  SERVICES PROVIDED BY THE VOLUNTARY SECTOR....................................... 2-3
  ORGANIZATIONS ACTIVE IN DISASTER.. 2-8
  SUMMARY OF UNIT TWO.. 2-9

Unit Three: Collaboration and Partnerships 3-1
  INTRODUCTION 3-1
  BENEFITS OF COLLABORATION 3-1
  CHALLENGES TO COLLABORATION 3-2
  STRATEGIES FOR EFFECTIVE COLLABORATION.. 3-3
  ENTITIES THAT FOSTER COLLABORATION.. 3-5
  PARTNERS IN COLLABORATION 3-6
  COLLABORATION IN ACTION 3-7
  SUMMARY OF UNIT THREE 3-9

Unit Four: Evolving Trends of the Voluntary Sector 4-1
  INTRODUCTION 4-1
  EVOLVING TRENDS OF THE VOLUNTARY SECTOR 4-1

NEXT STEPS 4-4

SUMMARY OF UNIT FOUR 4-5

Appendix A: Acronyms A-1

Appendix B: State/Territory VOAD Toolkit B-1

Appendix C: Common Terms and Definitions C-1

Appendix D: Contacts D-1

Appendix E: Historical Timeline and Lessons Learned E-1

Appendix F: Volunteering Historical Timeline F-1

Appendix G: Final Exam G-1

Administrative Information

THE FEDERAL EMERGENCY MANAGEMENT AGENCY (FEMA)

FEMA, created on April 1, 1979, is the lead Federal government agency responsible for emergency management in the United States. The mission of FEMA is to support our citizens and first responders to ensure that as a Nation we work together to build, sustain, and improve our capability to prepare for, protect against, respond to, recover from, and mitigate all hazards. Further information on FEMA is available on the Internet at www.fema.gov.

EMERGENCY MANAGEMENT INSTITUTE (EMI)

Through its courses and integrated programs, EMI serves as the national focal point for the development and delivery of emergency management training to enhance the capabilities of State, local, tribal, and territorial government officials; volunteer organizations; FEMA's disaster workforce; other Federal agencies; and the public and private sectors to minimize the impact of disasters and emergencies on the American public. EMI curricula are structured to meet the needs of this diverse audience with an emphasis on separate organizations working together in all-hazards emergencies to save lives and protect property. Particular emphasis is placed on governing doctrine such as the National Response Framework (NRF), National Incident Management System (NIMS), and the National Preparedness Guidelines.

COURSE OVERVIEW

Target Audience

This Independent Study course is targeted to:

- Federal, State, local, tribal, and territorial emergency managers
- Voluntary organization emergency managers
- Local and community organizations and volunteers
- Other individuals interested in emergency management

All of these individuals are involved in emergency management activities and seek an understanding of the roles of voluntary organizations throughout the emergency management cycle.

Course Goals and Objectives

The overall goal of this Independent Study course is to increase awareness of the roles and responsibilities of voluntary organizations in emergency management. Voluntary organizations have helped meet the needs of individuals and communities affected by disasters since the 1800s. Today, they serve a critical role in the emergency management field from helping communities prepare for and mitigate the effects of disasters to providing immediate response and long-term recovery services. Without the support, dedication, and expertise of voluntary organizations, the needs of disaster-affected communities would not be met.

At the conclusion of this course, you should be able to:

1. Describe the unique capabilities of voluntary organizations.
2. Identify important historical milestones in the development of the role of disaster mission oriented voluntary organizations in emergency management in the United States.
3. Identify the roles and services that voluntary organizations, both those with a disaster program as well as those without a disaster program, may provide throughout the functions of emergency management.
4. Explain the importance of collaboration and coordination amongst voluntary organizations and between voluntary organizations and their emergency management partners.
5. Describe the entities that foster government/voluntary organization coordination throughout all functions of emergency management.
6. Discuss the evolving role of voluntary organizations in emergency management.
7. Discuss emerging organizations and develop contingency plans for collaborating with these organizations.

PURPOSE OF THIS COURSE

Recent disasters remind us how vulnerable we are as a society. In order to avoid further great losses to life and property, it is imperative that governmental and non-governmental, voluntary organizations be closely united and develop strong working relationships. Combining resources and applying them in a collaborative manner will help us develop disaster-resilient communities and prevent losses in the future. Strong collaboration will also lead to more effective disaster response and recovery activities. The first step in developing closer working relationships between governmental emergency management and non-governmental, voluntary organizations is to learn more about one another.

The purpose of *The Role of Voluntary Organizations in Emergency Management* course is twofold. First, it is intended to increase the level of awareness of Federal, State, local, tribal, and territorial emergency managers, and members of voluntary organizations, as well as the general public, about the roles of voluntary organizations in emergency management. Second, it is intended to encourage further collaboration between government and voluntary organizations in the emergency management arena. The subject matter is geared toward an introductory level. Readers are encouraged to explore more about the voluntary sector through additional resources listed throughout the appendices.

This Independent Study course addresses voluntary organizations whose chief missions include the provision of disaster mitigation, preparedness, response, and recovery services to individuals and families impacted by disaster. Course information includes members of established Voluntary Organizations Active in Disaster (VOAD), to include the State and local VOADs emerging across the country and the National Voluntary Organizations Active in Disaster (National VOAD). National VOAD provides support, guidance, conference forums, leadership development, and other technical assistance to its members. The VOAD movement is an open and inclusive movement and any non-profit organization committed to emergency management work that meets the basic membership criteria is welcome to join.

You will find certain key themes in much of the work of voluntary organizations. Overarching themes include:

- Service to the whole community, both rural and urban.

- An emphasis on capacity-building, whereby a disaster-affected community is encouraged to learn and grow from the disaster experience.

- The idea that all disasters are local and there will be a strong emphasis on local participation and leadership in decision-making and logistical support for recovery functions.

- Voluntary organizations provide for millions of people throughout the country to get involved in their communities to help themselves and the whole community.

- Emergency managers and VOADs work together to help citizens achieve a "new normal" given the dynamics of disasters in their communities. The new normal can be achieved through all phases of disaster, and prioritizes approaches that go beyond restoring what is lost or protecting what can be lost in a disaster, but doing so in a way that lessens the impacts of future disasters.

The expectation is that completing this Independent Study course will lead to:

- A better understanding of the roles and contributions of voluntary organizations.

- Closer and more effective working relationships among all emergency management.

- A higher level of public service to communities throughout the country—a common goal for both governmental and non-governmental organizations.

Course Organization

This course is organized into the following units:

- **Unit One:** Overview and History of Voluntary Organizations in Emergency Management
- **Unit Two:** Roles and Services of Voluntary Organizations in Emergency Management
- **Unit Three:** Collaboration and Partnerships
- **Unit Four:** Evolving Trends of the Voluntary Sector

The course also contains several appendices.

- **Appendix A:** Acronyms.
- **Appendix B:** State/Territory VOAD Toolkit
- **Appendix C:** Common Terms and Definitions
- **Appendix D:** Contacts
- **Appendix E:** Historical Timelines and Lessons Learned
- **Appendix F:** Volunteering Historical Timeline
- **Appendix G:** Final Exam

Unit One: Overview and History of Voluntary Organizations in Emergency Management

Objective:

1. Identify unique strengths of voluntary organizations in emergency management

In this unit, you will learn about:

- The unique strengths of voluntary organizations.

- Historical events that impacted the growth and development of the voluntary sector.

- Characteristics of voluntary organizations.

INTRODUCTION

History has taught us that in order to be successful in providing the best service for survivors, the voluntary organization must be present. In this unit, we will look at how the voluntary organization utilizes its strengths to attain success throughout previous disasters and how its ability to develop the right partnerships, be the community's voice, coordinate the needed services, and be one of the most trusted groups involved in emergency management has led to its success in providing services to the survivor. We also look at the strengths of the voluntary organization and how past disasters have led to successful partnerships.

UNIQUE STRENGTHS OF VOLUNTARY ORGANIZATIONS

Whether during response, recovery, mitigation, or preparedness, voluntary organizations bring many unique resources and assets to help communities and individuals. Discussed below are some unique strengths of voluntary organizations that make them such effective partners with the other providers of emergency management services.

Arrive First, Leave Last

Voluntary organizations, through their local affiliates, are often the first on the scene for a disaster. Because many organizations are community-based, they are able to mobilize quickly and provide immediate assistance such as feeding, sheltering, clothing, and debris removal for individuals and families. Voluntary organizations are traditionally on the scene prior to a Presidential declaration, and they continue to provide their services independent of a disaster declaration, consistent with resource availability and community need.

There are also a number of voluntary organizations that are involved in long-term recovery activities including rebuilding, cleanup, and mental health assistance. Some voluntary organizations focus solely on the long-term needs of communities. They may not respond immediately to the event, but these organizations often will continue to work on long-term activities for many years.

Trusted by the Public

Voluntary organizations are trusted because they:

- Have volunteers who are qualified to address the unique needs of the affected community
- Are considered "good stewards" of resources and donations
- Are skilled in listening to and respecting the privacy of confidential information
- Have the flexibility to respond to local needs
- Come from the local community

By serving as a critical link between the community and the government, voluntary organizations help promote a quick and efficient disaster relief effort. Trusted voluntary organizations can improve the delivery of services where fear or distrust can hinder survivor assistance.

Community-Based

Voluntary organizations are well grounded in the communities served. Often, volunteers within these organizations are friends and neighbors who are committed to community service independent of disasters. As a result of this relationship with the community, voluntary organizations are able to incorporate the values, priorities, and spirit of the community in their disaster relief efforts. Additionally, voluntary organizations are frequently able to identify specific individuals, families, or groups who have access or functional needs, which may be amplified during a disaster.

Flexible, Innovative, Resourceful, and Complimentary

Through a coordinated approach, disaster assistance programs play a crucial role in the recovery of disaster survivors. Through the concept of "Whole Community" government, private sector, voluntary organizations, and individuals support the recovery of survivors and communities from the beginning of a disaster through long-term recovery. Disaster survivors who receive government grants or loans and participate in a community-based long-term recovery case management process have a more successful recovery. Through the case management process, all resources available including skilled volunteer labor, donated goods, and services or materials, can be leveraged and more effectively managed.

Since voluntary organizations operate under different legal authorities than government agencies, they have flexibility to address a diverse array of needs. Their mission is driven by their membership. The organizational structures common to most voluntary organizations help ensure their programs reflect community needs. Because they rely on the trust of private donors and member support, voluntary organizations have a strong incentive to use their resources efficiently, which often fosters innovation. Since every disaster is local, successful disaster response and recovery efforts must reflect locally identified community needs and services. Voluntary organizations have the flexibility, innovation, and resourcefulness to "think outside of the box" and provide service to people in the most effective manner possible.

Throughout the emergency management cycle, voluntary organizations assist in a wide range of activities including damage assessment, mass feeding and sheltering, cleanup and debris removal, construction of temporary housing, and rebuilding private homes. Additionally, voluntary organizations have trained volunteers with unique skills that aren't provided by the government employees. For example, many of the faith-based organizations have clergy and other individuals who are specially trained in providing emotional and spiritual care to disaster survivors.

Capacity Building

A benefit of voluntary organizations' involvement in the emergency management process is that they provide opportunities and tools to a community for capacity building. This leads to the community becoming more self-sufficient and resilient.
Some examples are:

- Training and Education
- Organizational Leadership
- Self-Advocacy

Service Capabilities

Historically, volunteers have provided varied skills, abilities, and expertise to disaster response and recovery efforts. Voluntary organizations are diverse and exemplify the ability to identify needs and provide resources quickly and efficiently. Each individual organization, over time, has developed skills and specialized expertise in varied areas of service. The list of services available continues to change as new disasters present different challenges. Services include but are not limited to:

- Mass Care (Sheltering/Feeding)
- Legal Services
- Pet Sheltering
- Spiritual and Emotional Care
- Emergency Medicine

- Financial Assistance
- Case Management
- Cleanup
- Repair/Rebuild
- Transportation
- Bulk Supplies and Distribution
- Donations Management
- Casework
- Volunteer Management

THE ROLE OF VOLUNTARY ORGANIZATIONS IN HISTORICAL DISASTERS

For many decades, voluntary organizations have been on the scene of natural and manmade disasters to provide aid to individuals, families, and communities. From the Johnstown Floods of 1889 to Hurricane Sandy in 2012, voluntary organizations have been at the forefront of helping individuals and communities impacted by disasters. Appendix E has a listing of many disasters that highlight important stages in the evolution of voluntary agency support and assistance throughout U.S. history. Many important innovations such as the formation of National VOAD and the development of the National Donations Management Network (NDMN) can be traced to these events and the roles of voluntary organizations in disasters.

SUMMARY OF UNIT ONE

This unit provided an overview of the voluntary organization, the unique strengths of voluntary organizations, and how historical events impacted the growth and development of the voluntary sector. We saw how flexibility and innovation can allow the voluntary organization to address a diverse array of needs for the survivor as well as the importance of capacity building in emergency management. Finally, in this unit, we discussed how the voluntary organization's participation in historical disasters led to the formation of the National VOAD, a major accomplishment in emergency management's history.

Unit Two: Roles and Services of Voluntary Organizations in Emergency Management

Objectives:

1. Describe the overall roles of voluntary organizations in emergency management functions.

2. List various services that voluntary organizations may provide in emergency management functions.

In this unit, you will learn about:

- The overall roles of the voluntary sector.

- Specific roles and services provided by voluntary organizations.

- Organizations active in disaster.

INTRODUCTION

This unit looks at the roles of the voluntary sector that are necessary to understand how the voluntary organization facilitates assistance for the survivor. The unit starts by discussing the roles of the voluntary sector, the public law associated with the voluntary organization's involvement in emergency management, and the scope of services the volunteer organization provides. The unit goes on to provide a list of the strengths that voluntary organizations possess and also some of the resources that they utilize in providing services for the survivor.

ROLES OF THE VOLUNTARY SECTOR

Volunteers have been assisting disaster survivors since the beginning of time. Neighbor helping neighbor is the beginning of "Whole Community" efforts. Disaster is local; it begins locally and expands to regional, State, territorial, tribal, and Federal if additional resources are needed. Voluntary organizations in the United States of America, have provided organized services to disaster survivors beginning with the volunteer fire department established by Benjamin Franklin in 1736. Since those early beginnings, voluntary organizations providing disaster services have grown in numbers and added new and diverse services to survivors. Voluntary organizations provide services to survivors from early response activities including mass care, volunteer management, and debris removal through long-term recovery. They partner with and work alongside Federal, State, local, tribal, and territorial emergency management agencies providing services that supplement and strengthen the ability of the survivor to recover.

The Robert T. Stafford Disaster Relief and Emergency Assistance Act (Public Law 93-288) (aka Stafford Act) specifically has several sections that reference the roles of voluntary organizations such as:

Sec. 403. Essential Assistance (42 U.S.C. 5170b)

(a) In general - Federal agencies may on the direction of the President, provide assistance essential to meeting immediate threats to life and property resulting from a major disaster, as follows:

   (2) Medicine, durable medical equipment, food, and other consumables - Distributing or rendering through State and local governments, the American National Red Cross, the Salvation Army, the Mennonite Disaster Service, and other relief and disaster assistance organizations medicine, durable medical equipment, food, and other consumable supplies, and other services and assistance to disaster victims.

Scope of Services

Voluntary organizations provide a wide variety of services to individuals and communities impacted by disaster. The variety and nature of these services constantly evolve as providers enter and exit the emergency management field, new needs are identified, and lessons are learned. These activities fall under some broad categories:

- Life-Sustaining Assistance
- Volunteer Management
- Donations Management
- Pet Care
- Functional and Access Needs Assistance
- Recovery Assistance
- Training
- Advocacy

Length of Service Delivery

Voluntary organizations utilize the best practices of service delivery in disasters from the long history of civil and social service organizations. Section 1.1 described how voluntary organizations are the first ones on the scene and the last to leave during a disaster to help ensure survivors arrive at their new normal. This demonstrates the flexibility of voluntary organizations to provide wrap-around services to survivors to ensure sustained assistance when needed. For example, a food bank may support disaster feeding operations, while continuing its primary mission of providing assistance to alleviate hunger in the community.

Human Resources

The strength of voluntary organizations lies in their ability to galvanize and mobilize the good will and charitable contributions of citizens from all sectors of society. Voluntary organizations through their vast nationwide network of skilled affiliated volunteers have the capability to expand human resources as the needs of a disaster are identified. This steady stream of labor, special skills, resources, and organization is brought to bear to meet needs.

Material Resources

Voluntary organizations bring a variety of assets and resources to communities impacted by disasters. Beyond the direct provision of material resources, voluntary organizations also provide a great resource to impacted communities by helping to organize and manage donations, both where a need is identified and when the donation is unsolicited. Voluntary organizations also provide valuable technical assistance and subject matter expertise related to donations management to ensure best practices are adopted at the community level.

Funding

Voluntary organizations are primarily funded by charitable donations from individuals across the country. While voluntary organizations may receive some support from a disaster operation, this comprises a tiny share of the overall funding of voluntary organization activities. The benefit of this funding structure is it gives voluntary organizations greater flexibility to deliver assistance, particularly when limits to Federal assistance may leave the needs of survivors unmet.

SERVICES PROVIDED BY THE VOLUNTARY SECTOR

There are many and varied services provided by voluntary organizations following a disaster. These services include activities beginning with training, planning, and preparedness, and continuing with early response activities through long-term recovery. National VOAD members have developed points of consensus and guidance that recommend best practices. You can learn more at http://training.fema.gov/emiweb/cgi-shl/goodbye.aspx?url=http://www.nvoad.org/resource-center/.

A. **Disaster Planning and Preparedness:** Voluntary organizations work with communities before disasters to help them take steps to minimize the effects of disaster. Activities include:

- Cross-training between community-based volunteers and established disaster response organizations, offering opportunities to build relationships and learn about major response and recovery activities.

- Mitigation planning to develop and implement ways communities can lessen the effects of a disaster.

- Preparedness tools to help communities build a disaster kit, create a personal family disaster plan, and organize themselves.

- Disaster education as a way to prepare and inform by distributing educational materials and making presentations to community groups, schools, churches, and individuals.

- Developing and training cadres of individuals within the community that can provide translation and interpretation services to survivors.

- Voluntary organizations, in cooperation with local governments, can identify and provide outreach to targeted populations to plan and prepare for service delivery.

B. **Mass Care:** There is a variety of mass care activities including (but not limited to):

- Identifying, staffing, and setting up shelter facilities

- Fixed and mobile feeding of disaster survivors

- Services to support mass evacuation for those survivors who cannot remain in the area

- Support to individuals with service animals

- Emergency financial assistance

- Emergency comfort and hygiene kits

- Emergency medical needs assistance

- Cleanup kits

- Bulk distribution of food, water, blankets, heaters, baby needs, childcare products, and other disaster-specific items not available from retail outlets that may have been impacted by the event

- Emergency First Aid

- Family reunification services are provided to family members inside and outside the disaster-affected area

- Shower units can be provided to support volunteer efforts or to support sheltering activities

C. **Disaster Mental Health, Emotional and Spiritual Care**

   Mental Health Services

   Voluntary organizations provide training and operational services to address mental health needs following disasters. Services may include early psychological intervention, crisis counseling, and/or longer term behavioral or psychosocial counseling. Referrals can be provided to professionals for survivors who are in need of ongoing mental health services for pre-existing diagnosed mental health issues.

Emotional and Spiritual Care

Many voluntary organizations, particularly faith-based organizations, provide disaster-related emotional and spiritual services and training.

National VOAD member organizations have created and agree to abide by the Emotional and Spiritual Care Points of Consensus regarding provision of services and the resource, "Light Our Way" (available in English and Spanish). All documents can be found at: http://training.fema.gov/emiweb/cgi-shl/goodbye.aspx?url=http://www.nvoad.org/wp-content/uploads/dlm_uploads/2014/04/national_voad_disaster_spiritual_care_guidelines__final.pdf.

As an integral part of the pre-disaster community, local emotional and spiritual care providers and communities of faith are primary resources for post-disaster emotional and spiritual care. Because local communities of faith are uniquely equipped to provide healing care, any emotional and spiritual care services entering from outside of the community, support but do not substitute for local efforts. The principles of the National VOAD—cooperation, coordination, communication, and collaboration—are essential to the delivery of disaster emotional and spiritual care.

Care for the Caregiver

Voluntary organizations also provide services for relief workers to promote health and well-being. Support for caregivers promotes safety and maintains sustainability of the assistance effort.

D. Community Outreach

Voluntary organizations collaborate with the whole community to contact individuals, organizations, businesses, and churches to share information with them about the local disaster relief operation, determine community needs, and provide information and referral for services and support to assist.

E. Donations Management

Many voluntary organizations have their own internal systems for donations management for both cash and in-kind donations. The National Donations Management Network (NDMN) and the Multi-Agency Warehouse (MAW) provide systems to address receiving, transporting, warehousing, and distributing donations during disasters. Voluntary organizations work collaboratively with government agencies to address unsolicited donations of food, clothing, water, cleaning supplies, medical supplies, building materials, household goods, and other items.

F. Communications

Radio communication services are provided by voluntary organizations that utilize licensed amateur radio operators to provide emergency radio communication to fellow organizations and local government personnel. Technical Assistance is provided by voluntary organizations to provide telecommunications and information management systems support to the emergency management community.

G. Child Care

Voluntary organizations establish and professionally staff temporary childcare centers for disaster survivors. These services include working with the children to provide recreation, emotional, and educational support in a safe environment.

H. Pet Care/Sheltering

Many survivors report they will not leave their home if they have no place for pets. Survivors are more likely to seek safe shelter from a disaster if they can be reassured their pets will be cared for.

Voluntary organizations utilize trained volunteers to provide care for animals during disaster including rescue, sheltering, reunification, and grieving services for people who have lost pets.

I. Resource Coordination

Before, during, and after an emergency or disaster, voluntary organizations exercise the 4 Cs in the acquisition and use of personnel and materials resources. This information helps provide for the effective and efficient allocation of resources and helps reduce duplication of services.

J. Cleanup/Muckout

Voluntary organizations help individuals clean up, provide emergency repair, and remove debris from homes damaged or impacted by disaster by using skilled/trained volunteers, tools and equipment, and cleanup kits to support operations.

K. Volunteer Management

Voluntary organizations help manage unaffiliated volunteers as a service to impacted communities to avoid problems associated with unaffiliated volunteers. They arrange to connect these volunteers with organizations capable of utilizing their unique skills. They also provide logistical support and training to make the best use of unaffiliated volunteers.

During early response, volunteer management is a critical part of providing Muckout and emergency repairs to survivors. Voluntary organizations can match volunteer resources to survivor needs.

L. Disaster Casework

Disaster Casework (DCW) is a *short-term* program, occurring during the response and relief phases of disasters. It provides for urgently needed life-sustaining services such as safer shelter, food, clothing, and health needs that are the result of a disaster. DCW also facilitates a client's transition from the Response and Relief phase towards recovery, utilizing education, and resource referrals.

M. Damage Assessment

Voluntary organizations can offer programs that assist individuals and communities in recovery preparation and planning. For example, Construction Estimating utilizes trained volunteers to determine appropriate materials, skills, and time required for home construction to support recovery planning.

Additionally, Community Assessment of Unmet Needs is a program that employs trained volunteer teams to conduct door-to-door surveys of long-term recovery needs. The results become the property of the requesting community-based recovery organization as a computerized database. This data provides accurate statistics for case management and grant proposal preparation. Reports can provide estimated costs for recovery, prioritize cases based on vulnerability, and provide a detailed list of total needs. Limited translation services for Spanish are also available. The database provided is compatible with standard case management systems used for long-term recovery.

N. Disaster Case Management

Disaster Case Management (DCM) unlike Disaster Casework is a longer-term program where a trained disaster case manager assists a client in formulating a Disaster Recovery Plan. DCM is client-directed and serves to link clients to programs and services that may alleviate their disaster-caused unmet needs (such as housing, counseling, advocacy, etc.), that a client would not otherwise be able to easily access without such trained assistance in order to achieve a successful disaster recovery.

O. Rebuilding and Repair

As part of long-term recovery, voluntary organizations can provide skilled volunteers, funding, and building materials to assist survivors in meeting their unmet disaster-caused needs. This begins as part of a disaster case management process supported by long-term recovery groups and is limited to primary, owner-occupied residences.

P. Relocation Services

Voluntary organizations provide services to assist individuals and families moving from damaged areas to shelters and other temporary or permanent housing facilities. Some organizations provide additional funding to pay deposits for rent, utilities, and other initial expenses that are required.

Q. Other Services

National and State VOADs provide other valuable services depending on the needs of disaster survivors. Contact National VOAD and your State VOAD for more information on:

- Financial Assistance
- Financial Planning
- Funeral Services
- Transportation Services
- Mitigation Planning
- Organizational Mentoring and Training

ORGANIZATIONS ACTIVE IN DISASTER

Get familiar with organizations

Peace time is the best time to identify organizations that provide specific services and to build relationships with their key personnel. Find out from partners, visit http://training.fema.gov/emiweb/cgi-shl/goodbye.aspx?url=http://www.nvoad.org, or Google to find out the organizations that provide the following services and write their respective names (hint: the same organization can provide two or more services):

- Feeding   a)____________________, b)____________________
- Children Services   a)____________________, b)____________________
- Sheltering   a)____________________, b)____________________
- Crisis Counseling   a)____________________, b)____________________
- Spiritual Care   a)____________________, b)____________________
- Long-Term Recovery a)____________________, b)____________________

- Debris Removal   a)________________________, b)________________________

SUMMARY OF UNIT TWO

In this unit, we looked at the overall role of the voluntary organization in emergency management, each National VOAD member, and other voluntary organizations and the services they provide. The various services provided by voluntary organizations include:

- Disaster Mental Health, Emotional and Spiritual Care
- Community Outreach
- Resource Coordination
- Clean Up/Muckout
- Volunteer Management
- Disaster Casework
- Damage Management
- Disaster Case Management
- Relocation Services

Unit Three: Collaboration and Partnerships

Objectives:

1. Identify the benefits of voluntary organization collaboration.

2. List the challenges to and strategies for effective collaboration.

3. Indicate entities that foster collaboration (government/voluntary organization, voluntary organization/voluntary organization, voluntary organization/community organization) throughout the emergency management cycle.

In this unit, you will learn about:

- The benefits of collaboration

- Important partners in collaboration

- Strategies for effective collaboration

- Examples of collaboration in action

INTRODUCTION

The roles and services of voluntary organizations in emergency management will be successful only when organizations are willing and able to collaborate with one another and with other disaster relief organizations to accomplish common goals. In this unit, we see how neither voluntary organizations nor the government, working alone, can help the American public mitigate against, prepare for, respond to, and recover from disasters. Collaboration among all sectors of the emergency management community must begin during the Mitigation and Preparation phases and continue through the Response and Recovery phases.

BENEFITS OF COLLABORATION

Effective collaboration benefits both the providers and the recipients of disaster assistance by allowing services to be provided in the most effective manner possible while reducing duplication of benefits. When collaboration is working well, expertise and resources are shared between voluntary organizations, the government, and elements of the private sector. This collaboration among disaster relief providers increases creativity, responsiveness, and the ability to draw on varied resources in order to assist individuals and families in their recovery from a disaster.

Here are some of the most important benefits of collaboration identified by experienced disaster-service individuals:

Improved Service

Collaboration yields more effective and efficient service to the impacted community.

Less Confusion

Collaboration reduces the sense of chaos that accompanies a disaster.

Increased Understanding

Collaboration helps organizations learn more about each other and their unique roles and responsibilities during disasters.

Improved Relationships

Collaboration leads to better working relationships between Federal, State, local, tribal, and territorial governments, voluntary organizations, private businesses, and the general public.

Reduced Fragmentation of Services

Collaboration facilitates a holistic approach to emergency management and minimizes the likelihood that services will be provided in an ad hoc fashion.

Reduced Duplication of Services

Many disaster relief organizations provide the same or similar services. However, when organizations coordinate their time and resources, more needs are met and fewer resources are wasted.

Enhanced Problem-Solving

Collaboration allows for more effective problem-solving through open communication and the sharing of ideas.

Service to Diverse Populations

Each organization has ties to different populations in the community. When organizations choose to work together, more populations are served and it is less likely that individuals needing assistance will be missed.

CHALLENGES TO COLLABORATION

Government, private sector, and voluntary organizations have different motivations, and missions, and operate in different structures. The spectrum varies from hard and fast policies that require congressional action to affect change to one person that can change a policy by saying the words. Levels of, forms of, and expectations of accountability vary greatly from government to voluntary organizations. This can present challenges that need to be overcome, preferably before the chaos of a disaster.

Examples of challenges:

- Different styles of communication
- Unreconciled cultural differences, including organizational culture, political beliefs, lack of cultural understanding
- Different attitudes towards problem-solving
- Different decision-making styles/processes
- Legal/statutory issues
- Structure
- Technology
- Finance
- Varying geographic boundaries
- Differing missions/goals
- Staff turnover
- Lack of continuity

STRATEGIES FOR EFFECTIVE COLLABORATION

Individuals and organizations involved in emergency management often experience differences that create challenges for successful collaboration. Although these differences bring unique strengths and viewpoints to disaster operations, it is critical that disaster relief organizations understand and address these differences to ensure effective coordination. Strategies for overcoming some of the more common challenges are presented below.

Differing Goals and Priorities

- Learn about and respect each other's goals, priorities, and differences.
- Reach agreement on a common mission for the disaster relief operation.
- Align goals and priorities so disaster relief organizations work toward the common mission.

Role and Responsibility Uncertainty

- Meet and communicate regularly about each other's roles and services before, during, and after disasters.
- Maintain a central point of contact in your organization who can educate others about your roles and services.
- Distribute written information about your organization's mission, roles, and functions.
- Attend each other's conferences and training exercises.
- Take advantage of technological communication systems (e.g., e-mail, Internet).

Lack of Planning

- Meet on a regular basis before disaster strikes.
- Develop working relationships with other disaster relief organizations before disasters.
- Develop written plans of operation specifying each organization's role and responsibilities during disasters.
- Practice exercising these plans of operation.

Varying Levels of Experience

- Survivor service delivery benefits when experienced organizations collaborate with new organizations. Both organizations have the opportunity to improve service delivery by sharing best practices from established organizations and adopting new ideas and energy that new organizations can contribute.
- Experienced organizations should recognize and value creative ideas that emergent organizations bring forth.

Changes in Personnel/Volunteer Staff

- Open, effective communication with other organizations about changes in your organization's personnel promotes trust necessary to maintain effective operations.
- Make time for training and support, allowing successful transition for new personnel.
- Be patient with new people and help bring them up to speed.
- Share your lessons learned with new people to avoid repetition of mistakes. Share lessons learned and future potential challenges with new staff to prepare them to continue positive relationships.

Differing Organizational Cultures

One of the greatest challenges encountered in this environment is a common understanding among partners relating to the difference between assets, resources, tasking, and asking. Government structures have assets at their disposal that they deploy and operate by mission assignment, tasking, ordering, and directing. Governments may make a request for assets belonging to voluntary organizations or other non-governmental organizations for resources needed; and voluntary organizations may make a request of governments for assets to fulfill a mission, as appropriate, available, and needed. Clear understanding of the difference between asking and tasking, and the true meaning of partnership is: "working with you, not for you." This helps promote a better working environment between different organizational environments. Ways of doing business may differ among voluntary organizations and other organizations.

- Learn about each other's differences and attempt to identify and overcome biases. (Instead, learn about partners' missions, plans of operation, geographical territory, and other barriers to service, and develop procedures to overcome the barriers.)

- Show respect for different cultures.

- Adopt a give-and-take attitude.

- Develop formal coalitions such as Voluntary Organizations Active in Disaster (VOADs) at the State, regional, or local levels.

ENTITIES THAT FOSTER COLLABORATION

FEMA Voluntary Agency Liaisons

FEMA has Voluntary Agency Liaisons (VALs) based out of FEMA Headquarters, the regional offices, and disaster operations to foster a strong rapport between all of the voluntary organizations, State and local emergency management, and the FEMA regional offices. During disaster operations, additional VALs are activated to provide support to impacted areas. During non-operational periods, VALs continue to build/maintain relationships and enhance collaboration.

State and Local VOAD

A VOAD unites State and regional disaster relief providers to ensure more streamlined, effective service delivery to disaster-affected communities. VOADs' four-pronged approach allows individual organizations to maintain autonomy while working together to maximize efficiency through:

- Cooperation—By creating mutual trust and teamwork among member organizations, providing a platform for sharing of information.

- Communication—By serving as a clearinghouse for efficient dissemination of available services.

- Coordination—By ensuring maximum efficiency in service delivery and avoidance of duplication of efforts.

- Collaboration—By encouraging partnering in relief efforts and augmentation of asset and resource management to meet unmet needs.

Regular meetings allow opportunities for networking; developing relationships; education; developing a plan of operation; and sharing tools, resources, and expertise.

State and Local Emergency Management

States and many local emergency management agencies generally have a VAL or an individual identified in the emergency management structure or the State Emergency Management Plan as the lead contact to voluntary organizations. This individual will often have developed a relationship with and have knowledge of the capacity of State and local voluntary organizations. The individual's knowledge and support of voluntary organizations and other State partners is valuable in building a network of community resources and partners.

PARTNERS IN COLLABORATION

Private Sector

The private sector is a vital part of the emergency management team. We see the Nation's vast network of business, industry, academia, trade associations, and other non-governmental organizations as equal—and equally responsible—partners in every phase from Preparedness to Response and Recovery to Mitigation.

While the opportunities for working together are virtually unlimited, we know that there are practical considerations. Through public-private collaboration, government, voluntary organizations, and the private sector can:

- Enhance situational awareness.
- Improve decision-making.
- Access more resources and capabilities.
- Expand reach and access for disaster preparedness and relief communications.
- Improve coordination.
- Increase the effectiveness of emergency management efforts.
- Maintain strong relationships with the emergency management community built on mutual understanding of limits and regulations.
- Create more resilient communities and increase jurisdictional capacity to prevent, protect against, respond to, and recover from major incidents.

Community-Based Organizations:

- All communities have clubs, groups, and organizations who work to meet the everyday needs of the community and its residents.
- They vary in scope and mission, but when disasters strike, they often are among the first to offer assistance.
- They have a much greater local presence and are often connected to the most vulnerable in the community though not necessarily integrated into the emergency management structure.

Faith-Based Organizations:

- They include local churches, food banks, spiritual care, and after-school programs.
- They often stretch their resources to meet the new needs that arise due to disasters.
- Many participate in Long-Term Recovery Groups.
- They bring in a wealth of resources from their respective denominations, such as: their facilities serve as shelters and kitchens, leaders are often trained as crisis counselors and also provide spiritual care.

- They are often the most trusted organizations at the community level.

Other Federal Agencies

One entity or organization is not enough to meet the challenges posed by a catastrophic incident. In addition to the Federal Emergency Management Agency, there are several other partners at the Federal level that are part of the team in preparing for, protecting against, responding to, recovering from, and mitigating against all hazards. The National Response Framework (NRF) (http://www.fema.gov/national-response-framework) and The National Disaster Recovery Framework (NDRF) (http://www.fema.gov/pdf/recoveryframework/ndrf.pdf) foster a shared understanding of collective roles and responsibilities. They help us understand how we, as a Nation, coordinate, share information, and work together—which ultimately results in a more secure and resilient Nation.

EXERCISE: Go to the National VOAD website (http://training.fema.gov/emiweb/cgi-shl/goodbye.aspx?url=http://www.nvoad.org) and locate the "Disaster Spiritual Care Points of Consensus." Review this document and answer the following questions.

1. List four National VOAD member organizations likely to contribute to the development of this document.

2. Identify how these organizations could have challenges coming to consensus in terms of: ministering to people of different faiths and beliefs, delivering services to diverse populations, proselytizing, and protecting disaster survivors.

3. Which points of consensus help address the challenges identified in item 2?

COLLABORATION IN ACTION

Long-Term Recovery Groups (LTRGs)

In the sequence of disaster relief assistance, voluntary organizations and the local government are the first on the scene to provide emergency assistance to meet basic health and safety needs. Long-Term Recovery Groups are a coordinating body comprised of voluntary organizations and community-based organizations to address the long-term disaster-caused needs of individual families not met by Federal, State, local, tribal, and territorial or voluntary organization assistance.

For information on LTRG formation:
http://training.fema.gov/emiweb/cgi-shl/goodbye.aspx?url=http://www.nvoad.org/wp-content/uploads/2014/05/long_term_recovery_guide_-_final_2012.pdf

http://training.fema.gov/emiweb/cgi-shl/goodbye.aspx?url=http://cwserp.fatcow.com/sitebuildercontent/sitebuilderfiles/ltrmanual2009.pdf

Coordinated Assistance Network (CAN)

CAN (http://training.fema.gov/emiweb/cgi-shl/goodbye.aspx?url=http://can.org) is a web-based case management tool and a resource database. It exemplifies the collaboration of the Nation's leading disaster response organizations coming together to improve service delivery and resource management capabilities in disaster response and recovery. Using lessons learned, founding organizations realized the need to share information between organizations to improve resource management and more effectively provide case management to disaster survivors.

Volunteer and Donations Coordination Teams (VDCTs)

The concept of the Donations Coordination Team was developed to support the National Donations Management Strategy, adopted by the National Donations Steering Committee in 1993. This steering committee, which was convened by FEMA, included representatives from State, local, tribal, and territorial emergency management; voluntary organizations; and Federal agencies such as the Department of Defense, the Department of Transportation, General Services Administration, and the Department of State.

The National Donations Management Strategy outlines the basic process for managing donated goods and services during a disaster. Prior to the introduction of this strategy, most major disasters experienced "the disaster after the disaster." A chronic problem was the disaster area becoming clogged with goods that were unneeded, inappropriate, or poorly labeled and packaged. Offers made with the best intentions often added to and prolonged the suffering of disaster survivors by jamming distribution channels and overwhelming voluntary organizations. The National Donations Management Strategy is based on the following assumptions about donations management:

- Donations activities begin before a Federal declaration.

- Unsolicited goods and unaffiliated volunteers are the primary concern.

- Designated goods may be affected by State policies in disasters when roads and safety are impacted.

- State and local governments are ultimately in charge of managing unsolicited goods and unaffiliated volunteers, though a close working relationship with voluntary organizations is necessary.

- The Federal government and National VOAD are in supportive roles.

- The full use of voluntary organizations and community-based organizations in the donations management process is essential.

- Flexibility in the donations management process is necessary; there is no single way to manage unsolicited goods and services.

- A united and cooperative approach is necessary; no single organization can handle unsolicited goods and services.

- Cash to voluntary organizations is the preferred donation.

- Information management is essential for a successful operation.

The National Donations Management Strategy makes the best possible use of the compassionate, altruistic instincts of Americans, while at the same time providing the level of information and containment necessary to emergency managers. This strategy illustrates the kind of creative problem-solving that can result from collaborative efforts between the government and voluntary organizations.

Volunteer and Donations Management Coordination Team

In many disasters, it is necessary for voluntary organizations, community-based organizations, the government, and others to work together to address the incoming flow of unsolicited donated goods and unaffiliated volunteers. In such times, a team approach has proven to be the most effective way for managing donations. This team is often called the Donations Coordination Team (DCT).

The Donations Coordination Team is comprised of voluntary organizations and government representatives; its mission is strictly to manage unsolicited donated goods and spontaneous volunteers coming into the disaster area. This mission is based on the premise that the public's involvement and support of voluntary organizations with in-kind and cash donations are critical for a steady recovery from the disaster. Emergency managers, both in the voluntary sector and the government, must be prepared to work with the public to ensure that their contributions meet the affected community's needs. Otherwise, unsolicited goods may be counterproductive, causing considerable waste of warehouse space, labor, and other local resources.

National Mass Care Strategy

The National Mass Care Strategy (http://www.fema.gov/national-mass-care-strategy) was introduced and developed through a collaborative process led by the American Red Cross, the Federal Emergency Management Agency, and the National Voluntary Organizations Active in Disaster under the direction of the National Mass Care Council. The National Mass Care Strategy recognizes that every stakeholder brings distinctive strengths critical to the effective delivery of mass care services and that the most successful mass care is achieved through collaborative whole community effort.

SUMMARY OF UNIT THREE

Collaboration is the process by which two or more entities make a formal and sustained commitment to work together on a common mission. Successful collaboration requires:

- A commitment to participate in shared decision making.
- The willingness to share information, resources, and tasks in the interest of a common goal.
- Respect for each other's mission and diversity.
- A sense of community.

The importance of coordination among voluntary organizations and between voluntary organizations and their emergency management partners was discussed throughout the unit. Some of the entities that foster collaboration are FEMA VALs, State and local VOAD, and the State and local emergency management. Community-based organizations, faith-based organizations, the private sector, and other Federal agencies are some partners that have worked successfully with the voluntary organization. The

Long-Term Recovery Groups and Volunteer and Donations Coordination Teams are resources that have successfully collaborated with voluntary organizations.

Unit Four: Evolving Trends of the Voluntary Sector

<u>Objective:</u>

1. Discuss the evolving trends impacting the voluntary sector in emergency management.

In this unit, you will:

- Learn about the evolving field of emergency management and trends impacting the voluntary sector.
- Summarize key points and course objectives.
- Discuss next steps.

INTRODUCTION

In emergency management, change is a constant that continues to drive success and the voluntary organization consistently demonstrates how this is done. In this unit, we will look at how every disaster can give rise to a change in how the voluntary organization meets the needs of the disaster survivors, and also how the voluntary organization functions in non-federally declared disasters, funding, and volunteer credentialing. Then there will be a review of key points of the course and next steps for the voluntary organization.

EVOLVING TRENDS OF THE VOLUNTARY SECTOR

Just as no two disasters are the same, the role of voluntary organizations is constantly changing to meet the needs of communities and disaster survivors. Several factors play a part in the ever-evolving role of voluntary organizations including:

- Organizations and personnel entering and exiting the field.
- Lessons learned from previous disasters.
- New laws at all levels of government that affect service delivery.
- Demographic and cultural shifts that affect impacted communities.
- Unprecedented challenges that arrive during a disaster.

Voluntary organizations work with government officials, businesses, survivors, and other voluntary organizations to best identify new challenges and to make the necessary adjustments to ensure appropriate changes are made to maximize service delivery.

Catastrophic Planning

Voluntary organizations are an integral part of any catastrophic plan. Engaging voluntary organizations in the catastrophic planning process can yield several positive benefits:

- It helps realize the best practices of whole community planning.

- Voluntary organizations are already embedded into communities, helping to disseminate the disaster preparedness message to residents of different communities and cultures.

- Voluntary organizations, with their unique authority and service-oriented mission, can help identify areas of need that may be missed by emergency managers.

Non-Federally Declared Disasters (Non-Stafford Act events)

Appendix E offers some examples of different disasters that highlighted the role of voluntary organizations and includes events where there was no Federal disaster declaration. The role of voluntary organizations actually becomes more critical during a non-Federal disaster. Non-Federal disasters include events where the damage may not meet the impact criteria for a Presidential disaster declaration. This may also include events where legal authority for a disaster declaration is lacking and impact to a community is significant (such as the Deep Water Horizon Oil Spill or the 2010 Haitian Earthquake).

Funding

Voluntary organizations depend on the philanthropy of individuals and foundations to provide financial resources needed to support their missions. Faith-based and non-faith-based groups both depend on donations for funding, according to the statistics from the Center on Philanthropy (CoP) at Indiana University-Perdue University Indianapolis gathered since 2001.

Economic Trend on Donations

Disaster	Date of Event	Amount Donated Three weeks after event
Tropical Storm Sandy	October 2012	$219 million
Japanese Tsunami	March 2011	$188 million
Haiti	January 2010	$752 million
Katrina	August 2005	$1.3 billion
Indian Ocean Tsunami	December 2004	$610 million
9/11/01	September 2001	$876 million

Several factors can have an effect on donations:

http://digitalcommons.bryant.edu/cgi/viewcontent.cgi?article=1017&context=honors_finance

1. The strength of the economy.

    - https://www.stanford.edu/group/recessiontrends/cgi-bin/web/sites/all/themes/barron/pdf/CharitableGiving_fact_sheet.pdf

        - The Great Recession reduced total giving by 7.0% in 2008 and by another 6.2% in 2009.

        - Although giving increased slightly in 2010 (1.3%) and 2011 (0.9%), it still remains well below the 2007 level.

        - Americans are giving nearly the same proportion of their income as before. As a percentage of GDP, giving has fallen only slightly, declining from 2.1% in 2008 to 2.0% in 2009, 2010, and 2011.

        - There is some evidence that the decrease in total giving comes with a more diligent targeting of poverty-relevant causes. Total funding to food banks in 40 cities rose by 2.2% from 2007 to 2008 and by 31.9% from 2008 to 2009.

2. The amount of press coverage and messaging.

3. The ability of the community to quickly organize.

4. The ability of the community to tell the story and identify the needs.

5. The number of events in a timeframe.

6. The perceived need of the population affected.

Volunteer Credentialing

Volunteer credentialing is a persistent issue during disasters that lacks an easy solution to questions of how States and communities ensure safety and regulate access to impacted areas. There is no national standard for volunteer credentialing. Each voluntary organization will establish its own criteria for volunteer credentialing and certification. Voluntary organizations are generally aware of credentialing issues including: training, certification, criminal background checks, privacy, and liability. Additionally, each State and community may have different statutes and regulations that may influence credentialing issues such as Good Samaritan laws. FEMA regional VALs and State VOADs are great resources to help address these questions and navigate local dynamics that may influence outcomes.

Please see these online resources for more information:

- http://training.fema.gov/emiweb/cgi-shl/goodbye.aspx?url=http://www.nvoad.org/wp-content/uploads/dlm_uploads/2014/04/state_and_territory_voad_lead_program.pdf

- http://www.fema.gov/pdf/donations/ManagingSpontaneousVolunteers.pdf

Social Media

Social media has become a critical part of the outreach strategy of many voluntary organizations. Media outlets such as Twitter, Facebook, YouTube, and blogs are important tools in helping to manage volunteers and donations, disseminate messages widely and at low cost, keep interested parties informed of activities, and build partnerships. As technology changes, voluntary organizations will continue to evolve and grow to ensure these changes help them use their limited funds to maximum effect.

Individuals and organizations working with voluntary organizations can take advantage of these opportunities to ensure effective communication and use these partnership-building technologies.

NEXT STEPS

Knowing your community

Voluntary organizations play a critical role in helping emergency management officials gain valuable situational awareness of the impacts and activities related to disasters in communities. Building relationships with these organizations can make the resources available to emergency managers and help stretch scarce resources. They can also help customize disaster assistance to the needs of the local community and ensure consistency with cultural norms and traditions.

Suggested additional trainings:

- IS-0244.b: Developing and Managing Volunteers
- IS-0100.b: Introduction to Incident Command System
- IS-0200.b: ICS for Single Resources and Initial Action Incidents
- IS-0700.a: National Incident Management System (NIMS) An Introduction
- IS-0800.b: National Response Framework, An Introduction
- IS-0806: Emergency Support Function (ESF) #6 – Mass Care, Emergency Assistance, Housing, and Human Services
- Pets course, other IS Mass Care courses
- Participation in national, State, and local exercises, drills, and evaluations
- Other training available in the community
- Training courses offered by voluntary organizations
- Community Emergency Response Teams (CERTs)

Getting Involved with VOAD

National Voluntary Organizations Active in Disaster (National VOAD) is a national level organization that supports groups that provide disaster services nationally. The core principles of the "4C's"—Cooperation, Communication, Coordination, and Collaboration—guide the organization.

One of the emergency management principles is "disaster is local;" with that in mind, there is also an opportunity to develop that same level of support on a State and regional level.

During a disaster is not a good time to develop the "4C's" and it is the best practice to have a VOAD in place long before an event. State and regional organizations do not need to have affiliation with a national organization. Most State and regional VOADs have some national organization members and additional members that reflect the community. Regular meetings allow opportunity for:

- Networking
- Developing relationships
- Sharing tools, resources, and expertise
- Training and informational briefings
- Developing a plan of operation

National VOAD is a great resource and offers support to help you get organized:

National Voluntary Organizations Active in Disaster
1501 Lee Highway, Suite 170
Arlington, VA 22209-1109
Main Line: (703) 778-5088
Fax: (703) 778-5091

SUMMARY OF UNIT FOUR

The role of the voluntary sector continues to evolve as the needs of the disaster survivors change and services provided expand. Ensuring that the voluntary organization is engaged early in the catastrophic process has proven to be very successful. During non-federally declared disasters, voluntary organization involvement is crucial to help secure funding and resources since Federal assistance is not usually available. Donations are a major source of funding to provide services for the survivors of disasters. For the Katrina disaster, $1.6 billion was donated 3 weeks after the event to assist survivors. The ability to raise funds is dependent on several factors to include press coverage, the community's ability to quickly organize, and the number of events in a timeframe. In order to maintain the voluntary organization's success in emergency management, it is important that organizations know the community, continue to train, and get involved with National VOAD.

Appendix A: Acronyms

http://www.fema.gov/pdf/plan/prepare/faatlist07_09.pdf

CAN: Coordinated Assistance Network

DCM: Disaster Case Management

DCW: Disaster Casework

ESF: Emergency Support Function

FEMA: Federal Emergency Management Agency

MAW: Multi-Agency Warehouse

MRE: Meals Ready to Eat

NDMN: National Donations Management Network

NGO: Non-Governmental Organizations

PPD: Presidential Policy Directive

SBA: Small Business Administration

VDCT: Volunteer and Donations Coordination Team

VOAD: Voluntary Organizations Active in Disaster

Appendix B: State/Territory VOAD Toolkit

There are useful tools on the National Voluntary Organizations Active in Disaster website to help in developing a State or regional VOAD (http://training.fema.gov/emiweb/cgi-shl/goodbye.aspx?url=http://www.nvoad.org).

A tool kit including sample bylaws and membership agreement can be found at this link: http://training.fema.gov/emiweb/cgi-shl/goodbye.aspx?url=http://www.nvoad.org/wp-content/uploads/dlm_uploads/2014/04/Bylaws-Template.pdf

Appendix C: Common Terms and Definitions

Affiliated Volunteers: A volunteer who is qualified and trained by, registered with, and accountable to a specific voluntary organization by its criteria and standards.

Capacity Building: A process by which an organization/community develops resources and infrastructure that increases the capability of the organization/community to meet its mission.

Care for the Caregiver: A process by which caregivers are given support and assistance (to include emotional and spiritual care) to help them sustain their contributions to a disaster operation.

Community Mental Health Care: The pre-existing community-based program that provides licensed mental health care assistance and treatment to residents in a community.

Crisis Counseling Grant Program: A Federally funded grant program to assist States with their disaster crisis counseling program.

Disaster Case Management Program: A Federally funded supplemental grant program administered by FEMA to assist States with their Disaster Case Management program.

Disaster Mental Health Care: A body of early psychological interventions designed both for groups and for individuals that mitigates acute distress while not interfering with natural recovery processes.

Emotional and Spiritual Care: Anything that nurtures the human spirit in coping with the crisis is emotional and spiritual care. This includes anything that assists an individual, family, or community in drawing upon their own spiritual perspective as a source of strength, hope, and healing.

Exterior Debris Removal: Typically, the removal of unwanted and damaged tree, vegetative, or other disaster debris from house sites, lawns, fields, and forests, and placing it in containers or in piles for disposal.

Final Cleaning and Sanitizing (post gutting, pre-mold treatment): The final and thorough cleaning of any remaining dried or wet remnants from the structure after gutting to prepare for mold control and treatment activities. Completion is typified by the absence of all nails, piles of dust/contaminates, standing water in the basement/crawlspace, and surfaces having been cleaned and rinsed of any dirt, mud, or other contaminants.

Interior Debris/Contents Removal: The removal of flood-affected personal items, appliances, fixtures, and any other items that are not structural components of the home that were submerged or damaged by floodwaters. This step is considered complete when all items to be discarded have been removed from the structure and any remaining undamaged items are in a safe location.

Muckout: The removal of mud, muck, silt, and other typically semi-solid material from a home as a result of water inundation.

Pets: A companion animal kept in a home for pleasure and not a service animal. (See definition for service animal.)

Service Animal: Dogs that are individually trained to do work or perform tasks for people with disabilities. (*Source*: www.ada.gov/service_animals_2010.htm)

Unaffiliated Volunteers: An individual or group not affiliated with a disaster voluntary organization.

Appendix D: Contacts

FEMA Voluntary Agency Liaisons: http://www.fema.gov/voluntary-faith-based-community-based-organizations

National VOAD: http://training.fema.gov/emiweb/cgi-shl/goodbye.aspx?url=http://www.nvoad.org

International Association of Emergency Managers (IAEM):
http://training.fema.gov/emiweb/cgi-shl/goodbye.aspx?url=http://www.iaem.com

Appendix E: Historical Timeline and Lessons Learned

The Johnstown Flood (1889)

- The deadliest flood in U.S. history, May 31, 1889, Johnstown, Pennsylvania.
- Six to nine inches of rain poured into the Conemaugh River basin.
- The South Fork Dam burst.
- Water was rushing into factories, stores, and homes at 20 to 40 miles per hour.
- The final death toll was 2,209.

The Johnstown Flood was a major test for early disaster relief voluntary organizations such as the American Red Cross. This disaster challenged their ability to deal with a large-scale disaster. Voluntary relief teams found "thousands dead in the river beds, twenty thousand without food but for the Pittsburgh bread rations, and a cold rain which continued unbroken by sunshine for forty days." The American Red Cross set up food and water stations, provided medical care, and established mass shelters to house the disaster survivors.

Hurricane and Storm Surges in Galveston, Texas (1900)

- On September 8, 1900, a hurricane and more than 15-foot storm surges began hitting Galveston, Texas.
- The Category 4 hurricane killed 6,000 people.
- 5,000 were injured.
- 10,000 were left homeless.

The Salvation Army and other voluntary organizations set up a warehouse for the distribution of clothing, including one million donated clothing items. These organizations also established shelters for the homeless and provided relief to farmers by purchasing new plants and seeds. The Salvation Army sent officers from across America to go to the disaster site and provide spiritual counsel and assistance. Following the Galveston hurricane, the Salvation Army developed local, regional, and national disaster service programs. This represented the first time a voluntary organization developed a structure to deploy assets on a national basis in response to a disaster.

San Francisco Earthquake (1906)

- A massive earthquake hit the city of San Francisco on April 18, 1906.
- 700 deaths; hundreds injured; 250,000 homeless.
- Fire erupted and spread through the city.

- The U.S. Army, voluntary organizations, and citizens' relief groups worked together in what could be considered the first "Whole Community" relief effort.
- Tent cities for tens of thousands of disaster survivors were established and maintained for many months.
- Volunteers of America ran a special train to take orphaned children to safety. The aim of voluntary organizations was to encourage self-reliance.

Following this disaster, the American Red Cross realized the importance of focusing on the solicitation of monetary donations, rather than in-kind items, which were often times inappropriate for meeting the survivor needs.

Anchorage, Alaska, Earthquake (1964)

- On March 27, 1964, an earthquake with a magnitude of 9.2, the strongest North American earthquake ever recorded, hit Anchorage, Alaska.
- 131 people were killed—115 in Alaska and 16 in Oregon and California.
- The resulting tsunami, the largest ever to strike North America, destroyed Valdez, Alaska, and was responsible for the majority of deaths.
- Seiches (a sloshing of water back and forth in a small body of water like a boat harbor) was observed as far away as Louisiana, sinking a number of fishing boats.
- Oscillations in water height were reported as far away as South Africa.

The Federal Government and voluntary organizations rushed in to provide food, shelter, and clothing to disaster survivors. This disaster marked the beginning of more Federal involvement in the costly rehabilitation phase of disaster work. For example, shortly after the disaster, Congress passed legislation making funds available to pay off mortgages still owed by many of the disaster survivors.

Hurricane Camille (1969)

- Hurricane Camille was the second strongest Category 5 hurricane in 20th century U.S. history.
- With winds in excess of 200 mph and storm surge of 20 feet, Hurricane Camille struck Mississippi, Louisiana, and Alabama on Sunday night, August 17, 1969.
- Camille's path brought torrential rainfall from 12 to 27 inches falling in Virginia during a 3–5-hour period.
- 27 inches of rainfall were recorded in Nelson County, Virginia. The ensuing flash floods and mudslides killed 153 people.
- Hurricane Camille claimed the lives of 256 people and reduced buildings to rubble.

During this disaster, criticism arose from especially hard hit minority groups that voluntary organizations were providing uneven assistance because of socio-economic biases. In response to these criticisms, the American Red Cross established standardized guidelines for providing equal and fair assistance to everyone, regardless of their race, religion, or socio-economic position.

Hurricane Camille led to the formation of National Voluntary Organizations Active in Disaster (National VOAD). After Hurricane Camille, it became clear that voluntary organizations were responding to the needs of disaster survivors in a fragmented, uncoordinated manner. On July 15, 1970, representatives from seven national voluntary organizations came together around the 4C's—cooperation, communication, coordination, and collaboration—to form National VOAD. (http://training.fema.gov/emiweb/cgi-shl/goodbye.aspx?url=http://www.nvoad.org/about-us/our-history/)

Hurricane Hugo (1989)/Hurricane Andrew (1992)/The Midwest Floods (1993)

Hurricane Hugo

- Caused 34 fatalities (most by electrocution or drowning) in the Caribbean and 27 in South Carolina.

- Left nearly 100,000 homeless.

- Resulted in $10 billion (1989 USD) in damage overall, making it the most damaging hurricane ever recorded at the time; $7 billion was from the United States and Puerto Rico.

- This event caused FEMA to re-evaluate debris removal as an emergency protective measure that would grant voluntary organizations and responders access to residents to provide assistance.

Hurricane Andrew

- 41 fatalities.
- The storm also destroyed roughly 25,000 homes and damaged 100,000 more.
- 250,000 people were left temporarily homeless.
- Hurricane Andrew was the costliest storm in U.S. history to date.
    - $20 billion in damage in Florida.
    - $41 billion in buildings and crops in Louisiana and Mississippi.

The Midwest Floods

- More than 14,500 people took refuge in shelters set up by voluntary organizations.

- In all, some 47,000 families were affected.

These three events galvanized a change in the way voluntary organizations collaborated to address survivor needs that overwhelmed the capacity of government and individual organizations to meet those needs. Those needs include donations management, mass sheltering, and volunteer management.

During each event, voluntary organizations set up shelters for evacuees. It quickly became evident that the sheltering requirements for tens of thousands of residents were beyond their capacity. Again, voluntary organizations and the military worked together to provide temporary "life support centers" to accommodate large numbers of people. The problem of unsolicited goods also required significant military support in the receiving, storing, transporting, and distributing of these goods. These events prompted the first discussions and collaboration on creating a donations management structure. This collaboration with emergency management at all levels and the voluntary organizations led to the first serious effort to address what has become known as "the second disaster." FEMA, based on lessons learned from Hurricane Andrew, introduced the concept of a Donations Coordination Team complete with a Coordination Center, State-based donations hotlines, proactive press releases, intensive field logistics, donations intelligence, and effective coordination with the FEMA Voluntary Agency Liaison and other key emergency managers.

The Midwest Floods marked the first time that a comprehensive unsolicited donations coordination effort was introduced. As a result, much of the public in-kind contributions were found to be helpful to the overall relief effort, rather than causing the types of problems experienced in the recent past.

The concept of the Resource Coordination Committee/Unmet Needs Committee was implemented to a point never seen before during the Midwest Floods. More than 400 groups were organized through a collaborative effort of the American Red Cross, FEMA, the Church World Service, and the affected States. An unmet needs handbook (later becoming the NVOAD Long-Term Recovery Guide) http://training.fema.gov/emiweb/cgi-shl/goodbye.aspx?url=http://www.nvoad.org/wp-content/uploads/2014/05/long_term_recovery_guide_-_final_2012.pdf was developed.

During the Midwest Floods, it became abundantly clear to FEMA that mitigation should be a continuous process that exists independent of disaster declarations and as an integral part of all programs, including Individual Assistance, Public Assistance, and Response programs. The voluntary organizations showed a strong interest in mitigation and proved to be important advocates in this area.

The Oklahoma City Bombing (1995)

On April 19, 1995, around 9:05 a.m., just after parents had dropped their children off at day care at the Murrah Federal Office Building in Oklahoma City, a massive bomb destroyed half of the nine-story building. One hundred sixty-eight people were killed in the terrorist attack.

The Oklahoma City Bombing required the counseling skills of many voluntary organizations on a long-term basis for both disaster survivors and disaster relief workers. Following this disaster, several voluntary organizations (such as Church World Service and the Salvation Army) evaluated their roles in providing pastoral care/spiritual and emotional care following acts of terrorism in the United States.

Compassion Center (later Project Heartland), a locally organized family assistance center, was operational by 3:30 p.m. on the afternoon of the bombing and operated for 16 days. In cooperation with the American Red Cross, hundreds of clergy, police and military chaplains, and mental health professionals provided assistance. Cooperation and support from local government, local and national voluntary organizations, and the private sector made this service possible. Compassion Center staff began to recognize media representatives and first responders as secondary victims due to long work hours and prolonged exposure to the survivors and stressed rescuers. At the same time, it also recognized the potential need to shelter the survivors from the media.

Hurricane Marilyn (1995)

During the hurricane season of 1995, 21 hurricanes battered the Florida and Alabama coastline, forcing many residents from their homes. Hurricane Marilyn, which struck the Caribbean on September 14 and caused damage to Puerto Rico, St. Thomas, and St. Croix, was the most costly storm of all.

During Hurricane Marilyn, there was a unique level of government/voluntary agency coordination. For example, 2 weeks into the disaster, Adventist Community Services took over the coordination of warehousing and distributing of some Federal relief supplies. Mennonite Disaster Services, Church of the Brethren, and Christian Reformed World Relief Committee (now World Renew) installed platforms for tents on disaster survivor properties to transition shelter populations into more sustainable facilities. FEMA supported this effort by providing ground transportation, building supplies, and equipment. For example, FEMA provided air transportation for the leaders of several voluntary organizations into the disaster area.

9-11-2001 Attacks at World Trade Center, Pentagon, and United Airlines Flight 93

Two planes were intentionally flown into the North and South towers of the World Trade center, collapsing both towers in less than 2 hours. A third plane was flown into the west side of the Pentagon. A fourth plane was hijacked with the intent to fly into the U.S. Capitol Building and was stopped by passengers in an attempt to take control of the plane, which ultimately crashed in Pennsylvania. Nearly 3,000 people died in the attacks, including all 227 civilians and the 19 hijackers aboard the 4 planes. These statistics give a view of the issues resulting from the event:

- Estimated units of blood donated to the New York Blood Center: 36,000.

- Total units of donated blood actually used: 258.

- Jobs lost in New York owing to the attacks: 146,100.

- Estimated amount donated to 9/11 charities: $1.4 billion.

- Estimated amount of money raised for funds dedicated to NYPD and FDNY families: $500 million.

- Apartments in lower Manhattan eligible for asbestos cleanup: 23,000.

- Estimated number of New Yorkers suffering from post-traumatic stress disorder as a result of 9/11: 422,000.

The events of September 11, 2001, occasioned an outpouring of giving that was unprecedented. Donations flowed into voluntary organizations local and national, large and small, new and well established at a rate that was staggering. Because so many and varied organizations were receiving such large infusions of cash, there were concerns that all the funds might not be used to provide direct assistance to the survivors. One of the lessons learned from the Oklahoma City Bombing was that spending all the money donated in the beginning left no funding for the long-term mental health services needed. Out of an abundance of caution, many organizations began to hold money for future perceived needs. It soon became clear that there were different ideas and definitions of assistance. In December, the 9/11 United Services Group (USG), with Robert J. Hurst of Goldman Sachs as the CEO, was formed. The organization was established to oversee and help organizations that assisted people affected by 9/11 be more effective. One of the tools developed to assist in better coordination of efforts and protect the privacy of survivors was a database, which later became the Coordinated Assistance Network (http://training.fema.gov/emiweb/cgi-shl/goodbye.aspx?url=http://can.org), a tool that has become invaluable to an effective case management process.

Challenges for service provisions continued to surface for years. Attempts to provide relief became more complicated, presenting some unique opportunities to define who was affected by this event. Voluntary organizations and emergency managers began to examine who was affected by disasters and revealed some other needs that had not before been encountered. Examples of new challenges:

- Compensation to survivors for trauma.

- Assistance for those who were unemployed for extended periods of time by the event.

- Addressing economic impacts to the transportation, tourism, and service industries.

- Assisting with urgent and long-term mental and physical health needs.

Spiritual and Emotional Care was one of the most critical services provided to survivors of the event. One example of the kind of care provided is St. Paul's Chapel, which stands in the shadows of the Twin Towers. It became a respite center beginning the day of the event and continuing for the next 8 months. Thousands of volunteers provided respite care to first responders, volunteers, and construction workers. The variety of care provided revealed the importance of standard traditional services and presented opportunities for new avenues for care, such as serving meals, music, wound care, making beds, counseling, massage, prayer, comfort animals, etc. Based on the work done during and after by volunteers, the chapel continues to be a tourist destination and maintains a number of exhibits of the event.

Hurricane Katrina (2005)

At least 1,833 people died in the hurricane and flooding, making it the deadliest U.S. hurricane since the 1928 Okeechobee hurricane.

Survivors were evacuated to locations all over the United States, with neighboring Texas housing 300,000 evacuees.

FEMA provided housing assistance (Rental Assistance, Temporary Housing units, etc.) to more than 700,000 applicants—families.

There were many new challenges presented by this disaster, including relief activities being interrupted by violence, managing and tracking the numbers of evacuees, challenges of evacuating vulnerable populations like critically ill and seniors, volunteer housing, and infrastructure repair.

Financial donations, goods, and volunteers were collected and distributed at unprecedented levels. Donations from foreign governments provided funding for Katrina Aid Today, a coalition of voluntary organizations formed to provide Disaster Case Management.

The Post-Katrina Emergency Management Reform Act (PKEMRA) allows more flexibility in assisting disaster-impacted communities (http://www.gpo.gov/fdsys/pkg/PLAW-109publ295/pdf/PLAW-109publ295.pdf)

Costliest U.S. Atlantic hurricanes

Cost refers to total estimated property damage

Rank	Hurricane	Season	Damages
1	**Katrina**	2005	$108 billion
2	Sandy	2012	$75 billion
3	Ike	2008	$29.5 billion
4	Andrew	1992	$26.5 billion
5	Wilma	2005	$20.6 billion
6	Ivan	2004	$18.8 billion
7	Irene	2011	$15.6 billion
8	Charley	2004	$15.1 billion
9	Rita	2005	$12 billion
10	Frances	2004	$9.51 billion
Source: National Hurricane Center[2][78]			

Voluntary organizations developed new programs and processes to deal with disasters of this magnitude. Volunteer housing challenges were addressed by establishing volunteer villages; new programs were implemented for tracking and reunification of evacuees; and new processes were developed to provide service to survivors relocated outside a disaster-affected community.

Haiti Earthquake (2010)

January 12, 2010, a 7.0 earthquake occurred in Haiti; by January 24, the death toll reached 316,000; 300,000 were injured; and at least 1 million people were homeless. There was a huge outpouring of relief from all over the world. Many voluntary organizations having domestic and foreign programs with a presence in Haiti provided a vehicle to begin relief efforts. There was catastrophic infrastructure failure. Relief efforts included providing fresh drinking water and emergency medical care. Rebuilding infrastructure to support relief efforts became a priority. FEMA and National VOAD provided support and technical assistance to the State Department and USAID and served as liaisons to bridge communication gaps and connect VOAD organizations to appropriate Cluster contacts. Together, foreign aid organizations working with domestic partners and counterparts were able to provide relief and recovery support.

Social media and satellite were used as never before to provide real-time information to support relief organizations and for funding opportunities.

Many Haitians were granted Temporary Protected Status, allowing local voluntary organizations, State agencies in South Florida, and the U.S. government agencies to begin "Operation Vigilant Sentry" to receive refugees and assist them in getting temporary living situations with relatives or sponsors in the United States. Voluntary organizations provided support to the effort including shelter, food, clothing, comfort kits, and, in some cases, transportation to new living situations.

Super Storm Sandy (October 29, 2013)

This storm affected 24 States, including the entire East Coast, with a variety of weather conditions to include blizzards, flooding, high wind, chemical spills, power outages, etc. Damage from the storm is more than $65 billion. At the peak of the storm, 2,000,000 people were without power. Power outages and fuel shortages continued for months.

Voluntary organizations, private sector, and government responders faced some unique challenges responding in an urban, heavily populated environment. Some of the challenges included available housing for volunteers and survivors, providing services to survivors in high-rise buildings having no elevator service, and high numbers of homes without heat.

In New Jersey, a statute banned younger teens from construction work, part of the State's child labor laws and regulations, making it problematic for youth volunteer teams to participate in recovery efforts. This statute is part of the same law that prohibits anyone under age 18 from working at a mine or quarry or using heavy machinery in various capacities, and limits employment related to alcohol. This issue has been identified as needing to be addressed by new legislation.

This page intentionally left blank.

Appendix F: Volunteering Historical Timeline

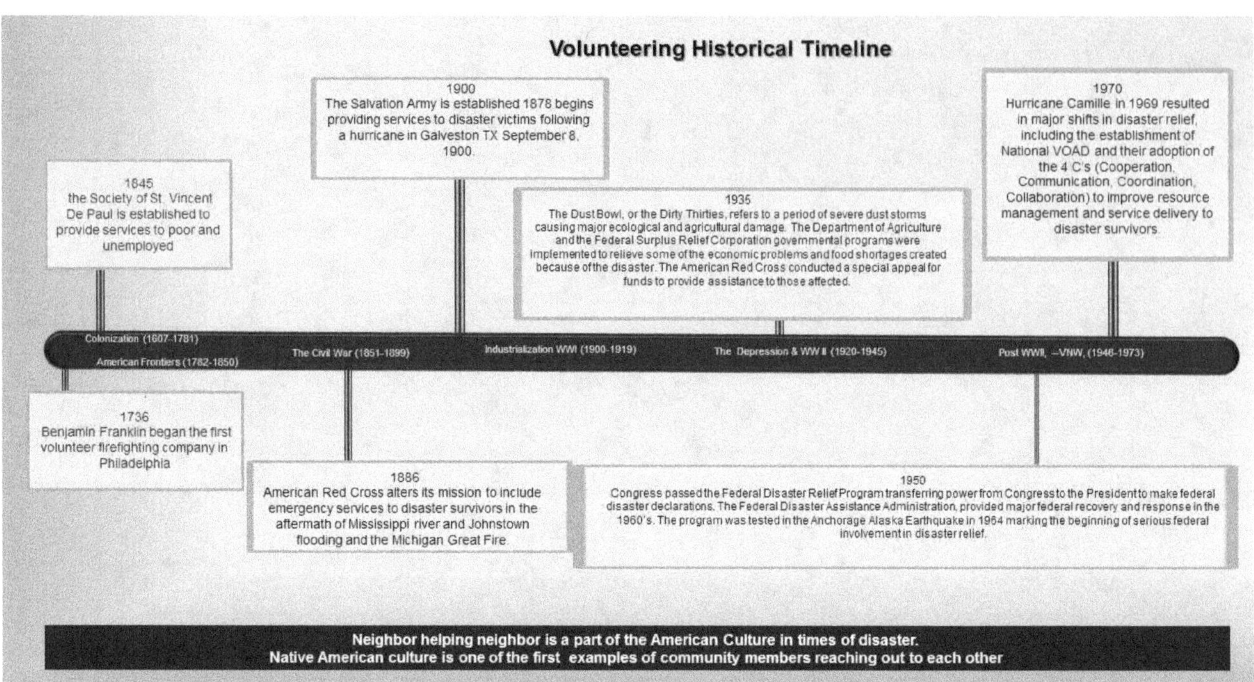

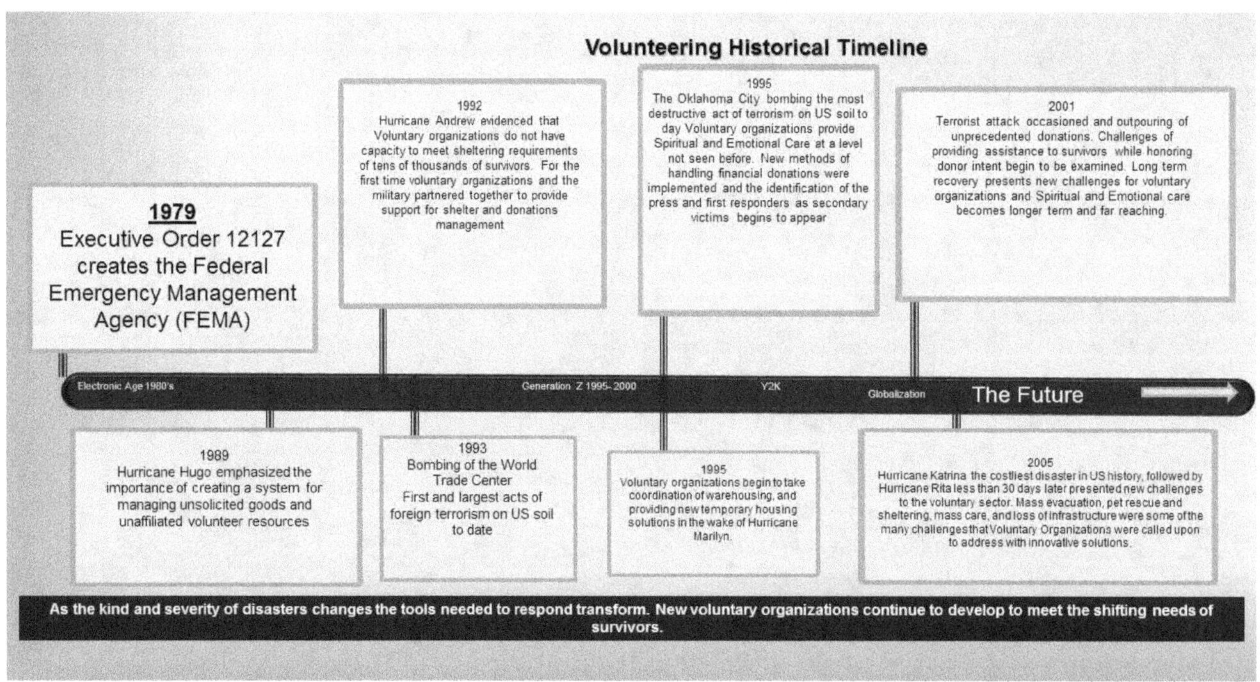

This page intentionally left blank.

Appendix G: Final Exam

Objective Unit 1

- Identify unique strengths of voluntary organizations in emergency management.

1. What does VOAD stand for:
   A. Volunteer Organizations Assisting in Disaster
   B. Voluntary Organizations Active in Drama
   C. Voluntary Associations in Disaster
   D. Voluntary Organizations Active in Disaster
   E. Volunteers Of American Disasters

2. Name a strength of voluntary organizations in emergency management:
   A. Arrive First, Leave Last
   B. Trusted by the Public
   C. Capacity Building
   D. Service Capabilities
   E. All of the Above

3. Voluntary organizations only respond to federally declared disasters.
   A. True
   B. False

4. Voluntary organizations operate under the same legal authorities as government agencies.
   A. True
   B. False

Objectives Unit 2

- Describe the overall roles of voluntary organizations in emergency management functions.
- List various services that voluntary organizations may provide in emergency management functions.

5. The Stafford Act specifically has several sections that reference the roles of voluntary organizations.

   A. True

   B. False

6. Voluntary organizations traditionally provide:

   A. Mass Care Services

   B. Furniture Repair

   C. Search and Rescue

   D. Business Grants

   E. Termite Treatment

7. Voluntary organizations end their disaster programs at the same time government disaster assistance concludes.

   A. True

   B. False

8. The National VOAD Emotional and Spiritual Care Committee developed a resource titled:

   A. Out of the Darkness

   B. Light Our Way

   C. Critical Incident Management for the Soul

   D. God in the Ruins

   E. The Sun Also Rises

9. Construction estimating is a program offered by certain voluntary organizations.

   A. True

   B. False

10. Which of the following services are <u>not</u> provided by the voluntary organizations?

    A. Financial Planning

    B. Funeral Services

    C. Law Enforcement

    D. Mitigation Planning

    E. Organizational Mentoring and Training

11. Voluntary organizations do not provide disaster relief services to:

    A. Individuals

    B. Pets

    C. First Responders

    D. Undocumented Workers

    E. Businesses

12. The best time to identify organizations that provide specific services and to build relationships with their key personnel is:

    A. Immediately after a disaster

    B. During peace time

    C. When a disaster is imminent

    D. During disaster recovery

    E. By accident

Objectives Unit 3

- Identify the benefits of voluntary organization collaboration.
- List the challenges to and strategies for effective collaboration.
- Indicate entities that foster collaboration (government/voluntary organization, voluntary organization/voluntary organization, voluntary organization/community organization) throughout the emergency management cycle.

13. What are the "4 Cs"?
    A. Cooperation, Communication, Coordination, Collaboration
    B. Cooperation, Communication, Confusion, Collaboration
    C. Cooperation, Communication, Coordination, Congeniality
    D. Consideration, Communication, Coordination, Collaboration
    E. Cooperation, Community, Coordination, Collaboration

14. What are the benefits of collaboration?
    A. Improved Service Delivery
    B. Improved Relationships
    C. Increased Fragmentation of Services
    D. Service to Selected Populations
    E. A and B

15. Which of the following is not a challenge to collaboration?
    A. Different styles of communication
    B. Unreconciled cultural differences including organizational culture, political beliefs, lack of cultural understanding
    C. Different attitudes towards problem-solving
    D. Mutual understanding
    E. Different decision-making styles/processes

16. The Private Sector is a partner in collaboration.
    A. True
    B. False

17. The Private Sector convenes all collaboration between the voluntary organizations and emergency managers.

    A. True

    B. False

18. Emergency managers have authority to direct voluntary organizational assets.

    A. True

    B. False

19. During non-operational periods, VALs continue to build/maintain relationships and enhance collaboration.

    A. Build relationships

    B. Maintain relationships

    C. Enhance collaboration

    D. Foster a strong rapport between voluntary organizations, Federal agencies, and emergency managers

    E. All of the above

20. Partners in collaboration include:

    A. Private Sector

    B. Faith-Based Organizations

    C. Community-Based Organizations

    D. All of the above

    E. None of the above

21. Other Federal Agencies participate in collaboration.

    A. True

    B. False

22. Collaboration in action does not include:

    A. LTRGs

    B. XYZs

    C. DCTs

    D. CAN

    E. VOAD

23. Donations arrive before a Federal disaster declaration.

    A. True

    B. False

24. The Mass Care Strategy was developed by:

    A. American Red Cross

    B. FEMA

    C. National VOAD

    D. National Mass Care Council

    E. All of the above

Objective Unit 4

- Discuss the evolving trends impacting the voluntary sector in emergency management.

25. Funding for voluntary organizations continues to increase regardless of the economy.

    A. True

    B. False

26. Which factor does <u>not</u> impact financial contributions to voluntary organizations?

    A. Perceived need of the affected populations

    B. Number of disaster events in a specific timeframe

    C. Ability of the community to quickly organize

    D. Amount of media coverage

    E. Personal desire to donate

27. Services delivered by voluntary organizations have not changed over time.

    A. True

    B. False

28. Social media plays an important role in the way the emergency management community communicates to the public.

    A. True

    B. False

www.ingramcontent.com/pod-product-compliance
Lightning Source LLC
Chambersburg PA
CBHW080814280726
48660CB00018B/3437